ANIMAL OLYMPICS

First published in the UK in 2020 by
Ivy Kids
An imprint of The Quarto Group
The Old Brewery
6 Blundell Street
London N7 9BH
United Kingdom
www.QuartoKnows.com

A CIP record for this book is available
from the Library of Congress.

ISBN: 978-1-78240-987-8

This book was conceived, designed, & produced by

Ivy Kids

58 West Street, Brighton BN1 2RA, United Kingdom

PUBLISHER	David Breuer
MANAGING EDITOR	Susie Behar
ART DIRECTOR	Hanri van Wyk
DESIGNER	Suzie Harrison
IN-HOUSE DESIGNER	Kate Haynes
PROJECT EDITOR	Claire Saunders
IN-HOUSE EDITORS	Lucy Menzies &
	Hannah Dove

Manufactured in Singapore, CO022020

1 3 5 7 9 10 8 6 4 2

ANIMAL
OLYMPICS

CARRON BROWN

ILLUSTRATED BY KATY TANIS

IVY KIDS

CONTENTS

WELCOME TO THE ANIMAL OLYMPICS

Animal athletes from across the globe have gathered to show off their skills. Some of the world's fastest, strongest, and most nimble animals will be competing in 12 exciting Olympic events, all aiming for the top prize: a gleaming gold medal.

It's not always the biggest, quickest, or strongest animal that wins our gold medal—sometimes we've chosen an animal that we feel shows Olympic spirit.

So, on your marks... get set... and off we go!

DIVING

These animal athletes are experts at diving and know how to make a splash. But which competitor will impress the judges and win the gold medal?

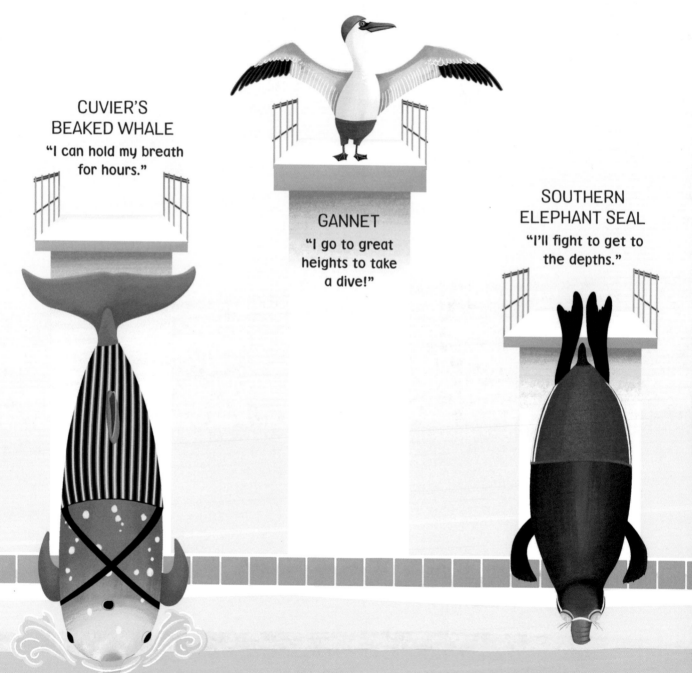

CUVIER'S BEAKED WHALE

"I can hold my breath for hours."

GANNET

"I go to great heights to take a dive!"

SOUTHERN ELEPHANT SEAL

"I'll fight to get to the depths."

Although GANNETS only dive around 32 feet into the sea when they hunt for fish, they begin their dive up to 130 feet above the sea's surface. Luckily, since they have no nostrils on their beaks, water can't rush in when they enter the sea at speeds of up to 62 miles per hour.

The SOUTHERN ELEPHANT SEAL spends most of its life in icy Antarctic waters. It can dive to a depth of around 1½ miles (that's over 450 times deeper than an Olympic diving pool) and can spend up to two hours underwater without taking a breath.

AND THE WINNER IS...

CUVIER'S BEAKED WHALES are the deepest divers—one has been spotted at 1¾ miles beneath the surface. They tuck their flippers into "pockets" (slight hollows) on their sides to make their body shape smooth for a deep dive. These whales can hold their breath for more than two hours.

SPRINTING

Blink and you'll miss them—these animals take the 100-meter sprint in their stride and leave humans way behind. But which animal will win the race?

PEREGRINE FALCON
"Watch out from above!"

CHEETAH
"You won't see me for dust."

OSTRICH
"I'm too big to fly, but look at me run!"

OSTRICHES are the fastest animals on two legs. These African birds can't fly, but they can run as fast as 43 miles per hour, covering up to 16 feet with every giant stride.

AND THE WINNER IS...

The fastest creature on the planet is the PEREGRINE FALCON, which reaches speeds of up to 242 miles per hour when it dives. It tucks its wings close to its body and zooms headfirst through the air to reach its prey.

With a top speed of 74 miles per hour over short distances, the CHEETAH is the fastest animal on land. This big cat uses its long tail to balance and steer as it sprints after antelope on the African grassland.

WEIGHTLIFTING

Roll up, roll up to meet the world's strongest animals. In this show of muscle and mass, which competitor is going to win the gold medal? Don't be fooled by their size—the largest animal isn't necessarily the strongest.

GORILLA
"Look at my huge muscles."

AFRICAN BUSH ELEPHANT
"I can easily lift more than either of you."

RHINOCEROS BEETLE
"Don't underestimate me—I'm small but super strong!"

The AFRICAN BUSH ELEPHANT is the largest animal on land. Its strong, muscular trunk can lift around 660 pounds. That's the weight of 750 cans of soup and is approximately a 20th of the elephant's body weight.

GORILLAS can lift up to 10 times their body weight. Their arms are so powerful because they walk on all four limbs and use their arms to bend and break off plants to eat. They live in forests in central Africa, and gobble up to 44 pounds of leaves, fruit, and stems each day.

1st

AND THE WINNER IS...

Some RHINOCEROS BEETLES can carry more than 100 times their body weight, which makes them our weightlifting champions. Male rhinoceros beetles have horns that they use to lift and throw other male beetles when fighting.

LONG JUMP

Whoosh! With one great leap on their powerful back legs, these animals launch themselves into the air, but which athlete can jump the farthest?

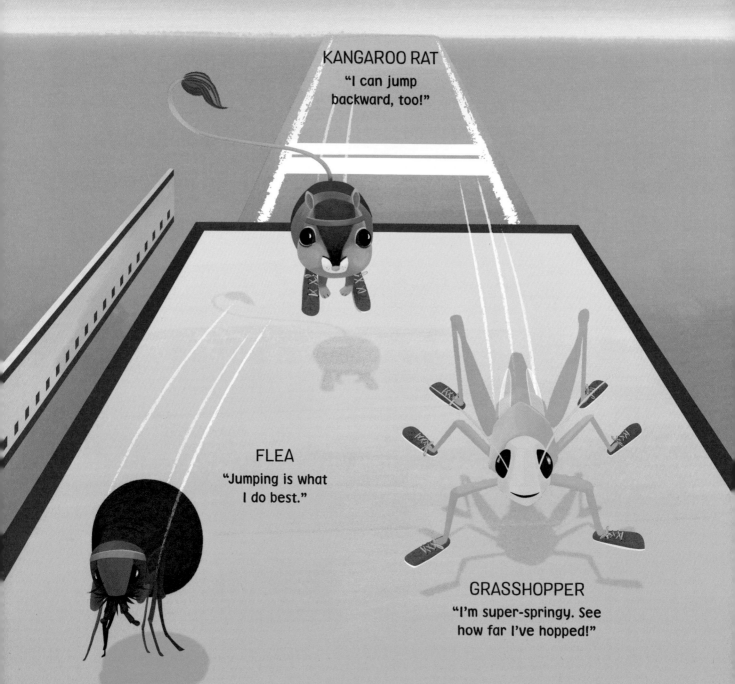

KANGAROO RAT

"I can jump backward, too!"

FLEA

"Jumping is what I do best."

GRASSHOPPER

"I'm super-springy. See how far I've hopped!"

Catapulting itself into the air, the GRASSHOPPER can jump up to 20 times the length of its body—that would be like you leaping from one end of an 82-foot swimming pool to the other. It uses the jump to give it a head start when flying away from danger.

KANGAROO RATS live in deserts in the USA, and have hairs on their feet to help them grip the sand. These small mammals can spring up to 20 times their body length and can even change direction mid-jump.

AND THE WINNER IS...

Using its strong back legs, the tiny FLEA can jump an incredible 200 times its body length. The insect leaps on to passing animals so it can feast on their blood.

1st

LONG-DISTANCE RUN

Many animals travel a long way each year to escape cold climates, find food, or search for a mate. These journeys are called migrations. Some of the distances traveled are huge; the animals migrate across whole continents and from one side of the world to the other. So which competitor will go the furthest in our long-distance race?

GRANT'S CARIBOU
"I can keep going for months."

ARCTIC TERN
"I could do this all over again!"

LEATHERBACK TURTLE
"Long distances are no problem for me."

FINISH

GRANT'S CARIBOU (a type of reindeer) make the longest migration by animals on land. They live mainly in Alaska, and move to different places in summer and in winter. Every year they travel around 2,983 miles, over mountains and through rivers and blizzards.

LEATHERBACK TURTLES travel thousands of miles on one of the longest ocean migrations. They hunt for their favorite food—jellyfish. The longest recorded journey of a leatherback turtle was 12,738 miles and lasted over 600 days.

AND THE WINNER IS...

ARCTIC TERNS avoid winter by chasing summer from one side of Earth to the other. They spend summer in the Arctic, then fly south to the Antarctic in time for summer there, before returning north. One tern has been tracked flying 59,650 miles in just one year.

BOXING

In the animal kingdom, lots of creatures fight to survive, catch food, and compete for mates. Most use sharp body parts, such as teeth, beaks, claws, and tusks, but a few animals actually box each other or their prey. The three animals in the ring below can really pack a punch. Let's take a look and see which gets top prize.

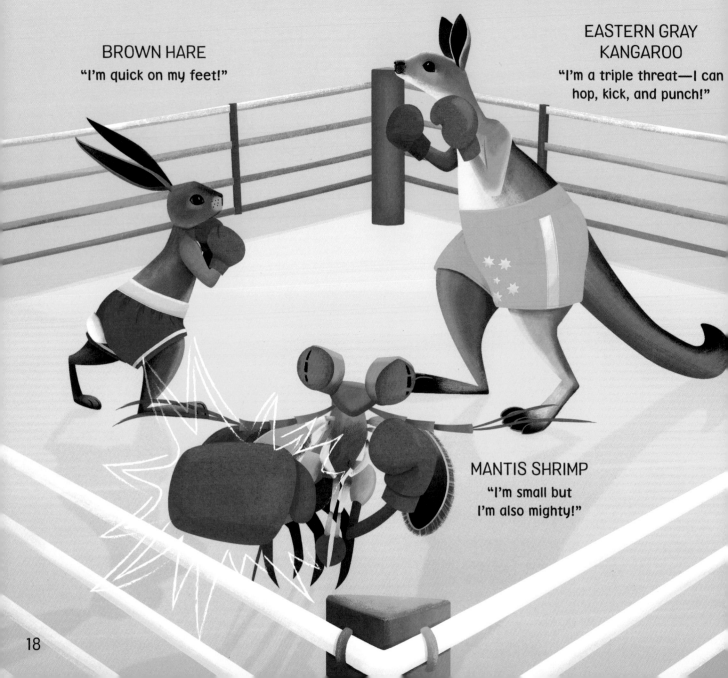

BROWN HARE

"I'm quick on my feet!"

EASTERN GRAY KANGAROO

"I'm a triple threat—I can hop, kick, and punch!"

MANTIS SHRIMP

"I'm small but I'm also mighty!"

BROWN HARES are found in Europe and Asia. The females fight the males during the spring mating season. They hop up on their hind legs and strike the males in the face to tell them to go away.

EASTERN GRAY KANGAROOS live on the grassy plains of Australia. The males settle disputes by slapping each other. They also rear up and kick both legs into each other's bellies.

AND THE WINNER IS...

MANTIS SHRIMP are tiny—only 4 inches long—but they definitely deserve top prize for the power of their punch in relation to their size. Their secret weapons are the speedy arms they whip out to strike and catch their prey. Each punch travels at about 75 feet per second. One of these shrimps even broke the glass in the aquarium it was kept in.

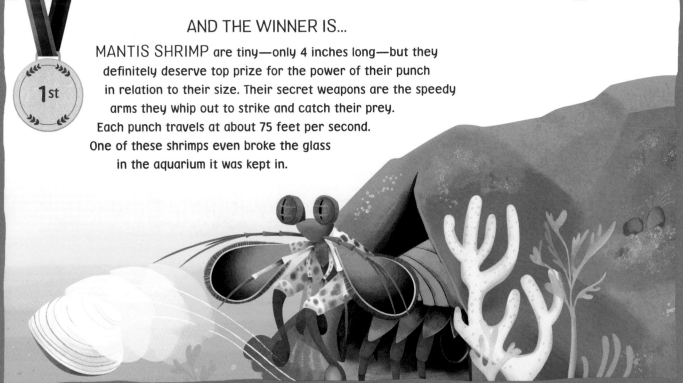

1st

19

HIGH JUMP

In the wild, jumping can get animals away from predators and out of trouble—or it can simply be a way of showing off. Let's meet the animal athletes with a spring in their step. Which animal can jump the highest and leap into the lead?

PUMA

"This is an easy jump for me."

SPRINGBOK

"I live up to my name—watch me SPRING into action!"

FROGHOPPER

"My hop is fast as well as high!"

The SPRINGBOK of southern Africa jumps up again and again with its legs straight and its back arched. This is a display called "pronking." Springboks may pronk to display their jumping skills, or they may just be jumping for joy—no one really knows for sure. They can jump around 13 feet high, which is more than three times their body length.

PUMAS (also known as cougars or mountain lions) are found in North, Central, and South America.

They can leap higher than any other cat—up to 18 feet, which is more than twice their body length. This helps them reach high-up cliff edges or tree branches in the mountains, deserts, and forests where they live.

AND THE WINNER IS...

The highest insect jumper is the common FROGHOPPER, which can spring 28 inches into the air—115 times its own body length. That would be like you leaping over 26 giraffes stood one on top of the other.

1st

The froghopper's back legs are powerful springs, accelerating it at speeds of 2½ miles per second into the air.

SWIMMING

Making a splash in the Olympic swimming pool below are a bird, a mammal, and a fish. Each one has its own unique swimming style, but which will be the fastest?

POLAR BEAR
"My big paws make great paddles."

BLACK MARLIN
"Whoosh! Beware my spearlike bill."

GENTOO PENGUIN
"I may waddle on land, but I whizz through water!"

The POLAR BEAR is an Arctic land-based mammal, but it's a strong swimmer. It swims at about 6¼ miles per hour, using only its front paws as paddles. Its back legs are held flat and used as a rudder. A thick layer of fat helps to keep the bear warm in the icy water.

GENTOO PENGUINS are the fastest birds underwater, zipping through the Antarctic ocean at up to 22 miles per hour. They dive into the water several hundred times a day to hunt for fish, squid, and krill.

1st

AND THE WINNER IS...

The BLACK MARLIN is the speediest creature in the water, traveling at up to 80 miles per hour—that's faster than a cheetah runs on land. As it zooms through a group of smaller fish in the waters of the Indian and Pacific oceans, it slashes its pointed, swordlike bill from side to side to stun and eat them.

CLIMBING

In the wild, the ability to climb keeps animals safe from dangers on the ground. Which of our expert climbers with a head for heights can watch their step and stay focused to win the top prize?

MOUNTAIN GOAT

"Look at my amazing balance!"

GECKO

"I don't need to use handholds."

GELADA BABOON

"I just love to hang around."

The GECKO has hundreds of microscopic hairs on its round toes that help its feet stick to surfaces. This means that this lizard can climb vertical walls and even hang upside down.

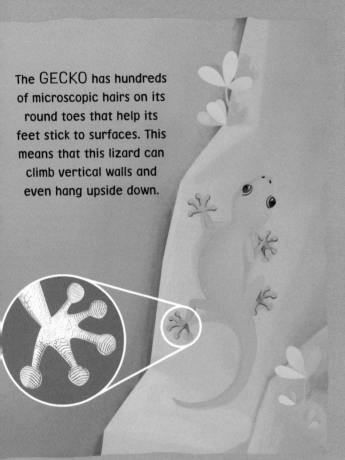

At night, GELADA BABOONS in Ethiopia, Africa, leave the high mountain plateaus and drop down steep cliffs to huddle together on ledges and sleep in safety. Their strong fingers help them to climb up and down the cliffs.

1st

AND THE WINNER IS...

When it comes to climbing, no animal does it better than the MOUNTAIN GOAT. Their special hooves have rough, grippy pads on the bottom, and two toes that can spread wide to help them balance. Not only can they clamber up almost vertical cliff faces, but they can make daredevil leaps from ledge to ledge.

25

WRESTLING

It's time for our competitors to step into the wrestling ring and put their strength and courage to the test. May the best and bravest beast win.

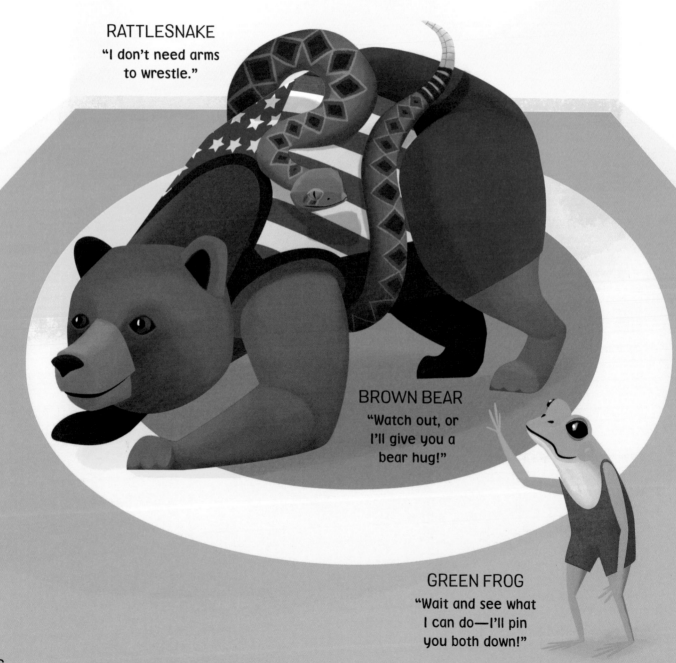

RATTLESNAKE
"I don't need arms to wrestle."

BROWN BEAR
"Watch out, or I'll give you a bear hug!"

GREEN FROG
"Wait and see what I can do—I'll pin you both down!"

Two male RATTLESNAKES will wrestle to breed with a female snake. Rising up into the air, they twist their bodies together, trying to knock their opponent to the ground. The defeated snake will slink away. These amazing animals are found in North, Central and South America.

BROWN BEARS live in North America and parts of Europe and Asia. The males fight over food or mates. They wrestle standing up, growling and roaring at each other. To leave a fight, a bear can lower its head and back away.

AND THE WINNER IS...

GREEN FROGS win because, like Olympic wrestlers, they actually pin down their defeated rival. Found in North America, they fight for territory, grappling with each other for several minutes until one is pinned down.

HURDLING

Animal hurdlers need to be good at both running and jumping over obstacles. In the wild, there are many obstacles to leap over, such as bushes, rocks, fallen trees, and waterways. Which of our hurdling competitors can run and jump their way to victory?

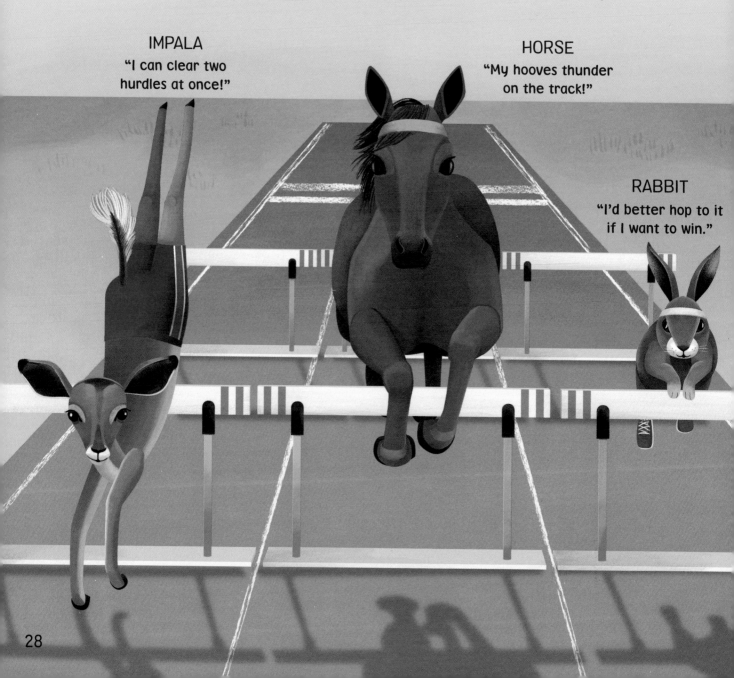

IMPALA
"I can clear two hurdles at once!"

HORSE
"My hooves thunder on the track!"

RABBIT
"I'd better hop to it if I want to win."

With the help of its powerful back legs, the RABBIT can jump up to 40 inches over objects and run in a zig-zag. This behavior confuses and slows down any animal that might be chasing it.

HORSES are excellent jumpers and can be trained to leap over hurdles. Hurdles are usually 3½ feet high, and horses can become skilled at leaping eight hurdles over a 2-mile course.

AND THE WINNER IS...

The IMPALA is a kind of antelope that lives in the African grassland. It is a quick runner and can leap a massive 33 feet forward and up to 10 feet high, clearing bushes to escape predators. Sensibly, it won't make a jump if it can't see where it is going to land.

GYMNASTICS

These flexible animal gymnasts know how to move their bodies. Their acrobatic tricks and tumbles help to keep them safe in real life, but how will they fare in the Olympic arena?

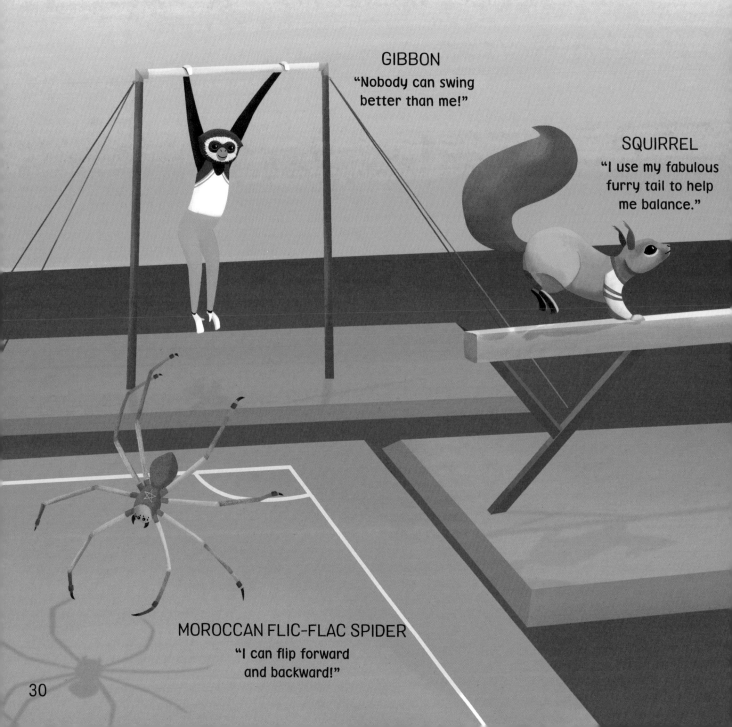

GIBBON
"Nobody can swing better than me!"

SQUIRREL
"I use my fabulous furry tail to help me balance."

MOROCCAN FLIC-FLAC SPIDER
"I can flip forward and backward!"

The MOROCCAN FLIC-FLAC SPIDER cartwheels across the desert using either backward or forward flips to roll uphill, downhill, or over straight ground. In this way, the spider can travel at twice its walking speed.

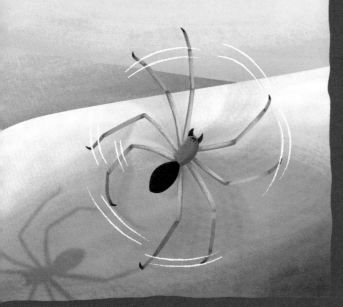

SQUIRRELS are quick and nimble, and can race along the narrowest of branches. Just as a human gymnast on a beam keeps their arms outstretched for balance, a squirrel moves its bushy tail to keep it steady as it scampers.

AND THE WINNER IS...

GIBBONS are true acrobats. They live in the forests of South-east Asia and rarely leave their treetop home, swinging hand by hand from branch to branch. They have arms that are one and a half times longer than their legs, and can cover a distance of 39 feet in one giant swing.

1st

DISCOVER MORE

ANIMALS

Amazing Animals
Guinness World Records, 2017

Animal Record Breakers by Steve Parker
Carlton Kids, 2018

Animal Records by Kathy Furgang and Sarah Wassner
National Geographic Kids, 2015

An Anthology of Intriguing Animals by Ben Hoare
DK Children, 2018

That's A Job: I like Animals... What Jobs are There?
by Steve Martin and Roberto Blefari
Ivy Kids, 2020

Migration: Incredible Animal Journeys by Mike Unwin and Jenni Desmond
Bloomsbury Children's Books, 2018

The Surprising Lives of Animals by Anna Claybourne and Stef Murphy
Ivy Kids, 2020

SPORTS AND THE OLYMPICS

Ancient to Modern: A Guide to the History of the Games by Joe Fullman
Wayland, 2016

Sportopedia: Explore More Than 50 Sports From Around the World
by Adam Skinner and Mark Long
Wide Eyed Editions, 2018

The Story of the Olympics by Richard Brassey
Orion Children's Books, 2016